This recipe book belongs to

purr-fect!

© Publication: LAPA Publishers,
a division of Penguin Random House South Africa (Pty) Ltd
Growthpoint Business Park, 162 Tonetti Street, Halfway House,
Ext. 7, Midrand
Tel.: 011 327 3550
Email: lapa@lapa.co.za

© Text: Lori-Ann Preston 2023
Illustrations by Tayla de Beer
Photography by Suzanne Loots
Food styling by Sybrand Harris
(The Cook and the Camera)
Title design by Renthia Buitendag
Proofread by Sean Fraser

Set by Renthia Buitendag

Printed by **novus** print, a division of Novus Holdings

FSC
MIX
Paper | Supporting
responsible forestry
FSC® C022948

First edition 2023

978 0 6370 0207 3 (printed book)
978 0 6370 0208 0 (ePub)

© All rights reserved. No part of this book may be reproduced in any manner without prior permission by the copyright holders.

A RECIPE BOOK!

What do MONSTERS & MERMAIDS munch?

Lori-Ann Preston

Illustrated by
Tayla de Beer

Colour me in!

www.lapa.co.za

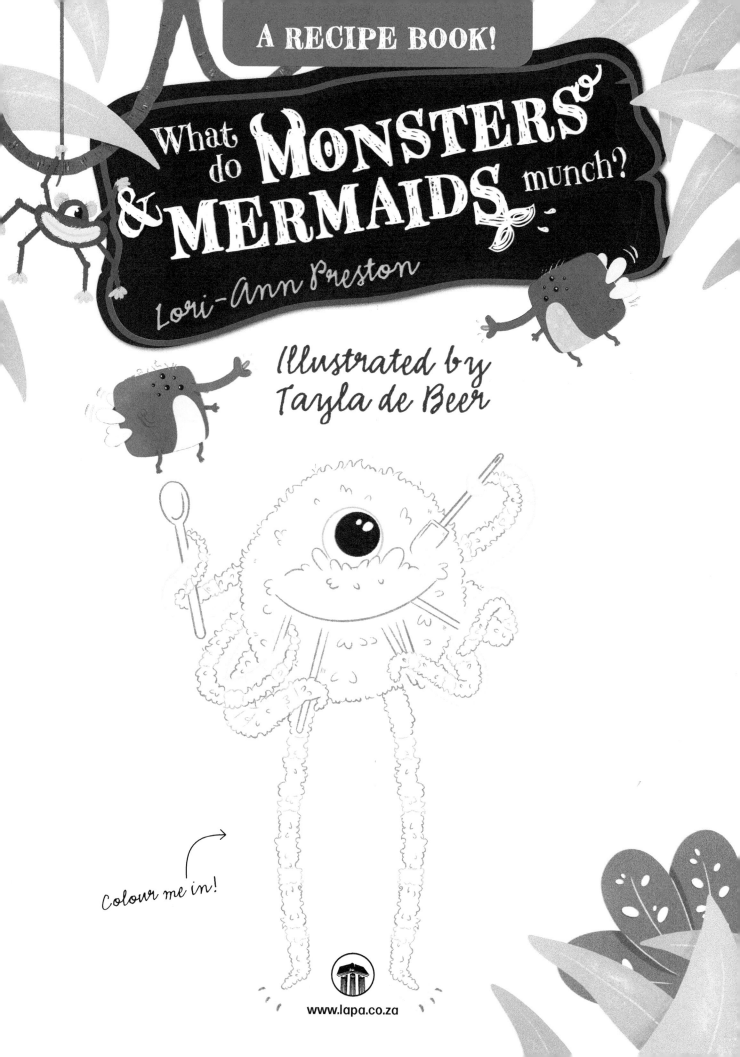

CONTENTS

TASTY TROLL GRUB

SCRUMPTIOUS SEA-CREATURE GOODIES

LEGENDARY LAND-CREATURE EATS

A NOTE FROM THE AUTHOR

Have you ever wondered what monsters and dragons like to eat? Could it be smelly toes or rotten chicken bones? Perhaps – and this is rather frightful – they like to suck on muddy worms, or to guzzle garbage covered in germs.

And what about unicorns, mermaids and purrmaids (half-cat/half-mermaid)? What are their favourite treats? Do they eat boring things like hay, seaweed and grass?

Finally, you can put your mind at ease. Fantasy creatures enjoy eating the exact same food that human children enjoy. In fact, they all have exceptionally healthy appetites.

For years and years, folk have been trying to get their hands on their favourite fantasy creature's recipes. Well, the wait is over. Today, the lucky person to find out their secrets is you!

In case you were wondering where all these creatures live, the answer is: Closer than you think! Monsters, unicorns, mermaids and a host of other special and magical creatures live on an island just off the coast of South Africa, called Picadeeda. It's a marvellous place.

I just know you're going to have loads of fun trying out these entertaining creatures' favourite recipes. Keep an eye out for magical and monstrous visitors. They may not be able to resist their favourite treats!

Xx Lori-Ann

P.S.

The recipes in this cookbook should be made by adults and children together. A kitchen is full of dangerous objects, especially stove tops, ovens and knives. Children should be closely supervised at all times. Some of the steps in the methods are not suitable for children to do alone. As an extra precaution, a (red circle) signals which steps are (NOT) safe for children to try on their own.

PICADEEDA
ISLAND

Name all the monsters from the recipes!

Colour me in!

BLOOBIDAHS' MELTED-CHEESE SANDWICH

Bloobidahs love anything cheesy. In fact, the cheesier, the better. While munching on a cheese sarmi, they love telling each other cheesy jokes.

Ingredients

2 slices bread of your choice
4 slices Cheddar or Gouda cheese
Margarine or butter
Tomato sauce → *to taste*

Method

1. Spread margarine or butter on both sides of the bread.
2. Smear tomato sauce on one slice of bread and place the cheese on top. Cover it with the other slice of bread.
3. Place a large dollop → *a little more than a tablespoon* of margarine or butter into a frying pan and then add your sandwich.
4. Keep turning the bread until it is crisp and golden-brown.

8

Colour me in!

Here are some cheesy jokes for you:

Knock, knock
Who's there?
Orange
Orange who?
Orange you going to open the door?

How do you make someone smile?
Tell them to: "Say cheese!"

What do you call cheese that isn't your own?
Nacho cheese.

9

Colour me in!

10

GOBBLE-DE-GOOK'S CHEESY PUFFS

Makes 6

Ingredients

1 cup cake flour
1 egg
3 tsp baking powder
2 cups grated Cheddar cheese
½ cup milk
Non-stick spray
Salt and pepper, to taste

Method

1. Preheat the oven to 200°C.
2. Sift the flour into a bowl.
3. In a separate bowl, whisk the egg.
4. Add all the ingredients together and gently mix.
5. Spray your muffin pan with non-stick spray.
6. Spoon the mixture into each of the muffin cases.
7. Bake for 12 minutes until puffed and golden.

Gobble-de-Gook, as his name suggests, is the greatest gobbler in the history of gobblers. Cheesy puffs are his favourite meal. He loves them so much that he eats them every day. Gobbling isn't recommended for children, as it causes stomach aches, but for Gobble-de-Gook, it's a perfectly acceptable behaviour. Gobble-de-Gook has six hands, which are perfect for gobbling. Gobble-de-Gook can finish six cheesy puffs in five seconds!

please don't try that at home.

Don't actually do that.

OKEY-DOKEY. READY? STEADY? GOBBLE!

YUMPET CRUMPETS

Yumpets are cool. Yumpets are trendy. Yumpets are famous for baking crumpets. Yumpets are extremely fashionable monsters. When they're not in the hair salon, trying out flashy new hairstyles, they can be found enjoying crumpets and tea. You can be stylish and cool too. All you have to do is bake and eat some of these scrumptious Yumpet crumpets.

Ingredients

1 cup cake flour
Pinch of salt
1 egg
1 tbsp white sugar
1 cup milk
1 tbsp butter, melted
2 tsp baking powder

 heaped!

**YAY! YAY! YUM!
LET'S HEAR IT
FOR YUMPETS
AND THEIR
CRUMPETS!**

Method

1. Sift the flour and salt together in a bowl.
2. Beat an egg in a separate bowl and place it to the side.
3. Make a well in the centre of the flour mixture. — *In other words, dig a hole.*
4. Place the sugar, well-beaten egg, and half of the milk into the well.
5. Mix well and beat the mixture to remove the lumps.
6. Add the remainder of the milk, followed by the butter and baking powder.
7. Mix it again.
8. Pour the mixture into a jug.
9. Heat a frying pan on the stove and grease it lightly, or spray it with non-stick.
10. Pour a little mixture into the pan to form a circle. When a few bubbles threaten to appear on top of your crumpet, flip it over. The second side will be ready soon after that.
11. Serve with a smearing of butter and jam or honey.

BOOPIE BANANA BREAD

Boopies are the cutest things you've ever seen. Boopies believe that every meal should be shared and enjoyed with friends and family. This banana bread recipe has been handed down from generation to generation of Boopies, and it is perfect for sharing. Why not give it a go?

Ingredients

1½ cups sugar
125g butter
2 eggs
3 cups flour
1 heaped tsp baking powder
1 tsp vanilla essence
1 tsp bicarbonate soda
4–5 mashed bananas
½ to ¾ cup milk
Non-stick spray

Method

1. Preheat oven to 180°C.
2. Cream sugar and butter.
   — *please note ...*
3. Beat and then add the eggs to the sugar mixture.
4. Add the rest of the ingredients to the bowl and mix them together.
5. Spray a bread dish with non-stick spray.
6. Pour the mixture into the dish.
7. Bake your banana bread in the oven for 1 hour.

There are two ways to cream butter and sugar:

- The professional way: Allow the butter to soften at room temperature. Add the sugar. Mix with an electric mixer.
- The monster way: Soften the butter in the microwave. Add the sugar. Stir with a wooden spoon.

Be like a Boopie, and share this bread with someone you like.

15

Be warned: Non-drum-players do not always appreciate drumming. But what is appreciated is the sound of Ghip crunchies being munched, chomped and crunched.

GHIP
CHOCOLATE CRUNCHIES

Ghips are very noisy monsters. They love being in the kitchen where they find wonderful things to bash and clang together. The whole of Picadeeda hears them in action when they bake. They start off by setting up a drumming station with pots and pans. They each grab a wooden spoon and begin to bang and bake.

It is certainly recommended that children do the same.

Ingredients

Method *Crunchie*

½ cup brown or white sugar
170g butter *at room temperature*

1 cup oats
1 tsp baking powder
1 cup cake flour
1 cup coconut
2 tsp cocoa powder
Non-stick spray

1. Preheat the oven to 190°C.
2. Cream the sugar and butter together.
3. Add all of the dry ingredients: Oats, baking powder, flour, coconut and cocoa powder.
4. Coat a baking pan with non-stick spray.
5. Press the mixture into the baking pan.
6. Bake in the oven for 20 minutes.
7. While the crunchie mixture is baking, prepare the icing.

Ingredients

Method *Icing*

2 cups icing sugar
4 tsp cocoa powder
½ tsp vanilla essence
4 tbsp hot water
2 tbsp melted butter

1. Beat all of the ingredients in a bowl until the mixture thickens.
2. Remove the crunchie mixture from the oven.
3. Pour the icing over the mixture while it's still hot. → *After it has baked.*
4. Leave the crunchies to set. When cool, cut them into squares.

 *Egg-joy!*

YOLKEY'S EGG-STRA-FUN SCRAMBLED EGG ON TOAST

Yolkey is ga-ga about eggs.
He only ever has eggs on the brain.

Ingredients

1 slice bread of your choice
1 egg
1 tsp butter
Salt and pepper, to taste

Method

1. Place a slice of bread in the toaster.
2. Heat a frying pan on a medium heat on the stove.
3. Crack the egg into the pan.
4. Add about a teaspoonful of butter.
5. Keep stirring the egg with a wooden spoon or spatula.
6. Spread butter or margarine on the toast. Place the egg on top. Add a sprinkling of salt and pepper.

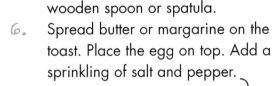 *If you choose.*

Let's have an interview with Yolkey!

What is your favourite colour?
Yolkey: Yellow.
What is your favourite thing to eat?
Yolkey: Eggs.
Why do you like eggs?
Yolkey: Because they are egg-citing and egg-straordinary.
Would you mind sharing your favourite egg recipes with us?
Yolkey: Yes! That is an egg-cellent idea. I think children will love this egg-sperience.

This is egg-citing!

HULLABALOO'S PEANUT-BUTTER COOKIES

Hullabaloo loves peanuts. Actually, it's peanut butter she loves most. Hullabaloo owns a peanut farm and factory just north of the city. The sandy soil on the island is ideal for peanut production.

Ingredients

½ cup butter *at room temperature*

1 cup brown sugar
½ cup peanut butter
1 tsp vanilla essence
1 egg
Non-stick spray
1 ¼ cups cake flour
¾ tsp baking powder

Method

1. Preheat the oven to 180°C.
2. Spray a baking tray with non-stick spray.
3. Cream the butter and sugar in a large bowl.
4. Add peanut butter to the butter and sugar and mix.
5. Add vanilla essence and mix.
6. Beat the egg in a separate bowl.
7. Add the beaten egg and mix.
8. Sift the flour and baking powder in a separate bowl.
9. Add the flour and baking powder and …

   yup, you guessed it, mix again.

10. Roll the dough into little balls and place them on a baking tray.
11. Flatten each ball with a fork.
12. Bake cookies for about 12–15 minutes, or until you see the colour start to change on the sides.
13. Allow the cookies to completely cool before removing them from the baking tray.

Some children love peanuts, but others don't enjoy them as much. I guess it all depends on your unique taste buds.

Humans have been baking this recipe for many, many years, but did you know it originated on Picadeeda Island? True story.

It isn't really, but let's pretend.

WACKY'S CHOCOLATE CAKE

You can't tell his legs from his arms.

This chocolatey-delicious cake was invented by Wacky. He has five arms and five legs! This may seem odd, but it's wonderful for a whacky monster. If you're wondering if you should try this recipe, the answer is 100% yes! Get going now!

Ingredients

2 cups cake flour
2 tsp bicarbonate soda
1 tsp salt
2 cups white sugar
6 tbsp cocoa powder
¼ cup sunflower oil
2 tbsp brown vinegar
2 tsp vanilla essence
2 cups water
Non-stick spray

Method, Cake

1. Preheat the oven to 180°C.
2. In a large bowl, sift the flour, bicarbonate of soda, salt, sugar and cocoa.
3. Add the oil, vinegar, vanilla essence and water to the dry ingredients.
4. Mix the ingredients together until a smooth consistency is formed.
5. Spray an oven-proof dish with non-stick spray.
6. Pour the mixture into the dish.
7. Bake for 1 hour.

Ingredients

500g icing sugar
½ cup margarine
5 tbsp milk
4 tsp cocoa powder
1 tsp vanilla essence

Method, Icing

1. Sift the icing sugar into a bowl.
2. Melt the margarine in a saucepan on the stove.
3. Add the milk and cocoa to the melted margarine.
4. Pour the margarine, milk and cocoa mix over the icing sugar and stir.
5. Add the vanilla essence to the mix and stir.
6. Pour the icing over the cake.

ROSY'S APPLE CRUMBLE

Unicorns stick together.
Especially when they catch a whiff of Rosy's mouthwatering
apple crumble baking in the oven. The warm, slightly sweet aroma
with a hint of spice can be smelled from miles away. The scent is like
inhaling a cuddle from your favourite person. The unicorns canter over
to Rosy's kitchen and huddle together in eager anticipation of placing
the yummy in their tummy.

Ingredients

**1 small can unsweetened
apple slices**
1 handful of raisins
  → *optional*

¼ tsp cinnamon
1 cup cake flour
½ cup white or brown sugar
2 tsp baking powder
1 egg
4 tbsp margarine
Non-stick spray

*preferably with
clean, washed
hands!*

Method

1. Preheat the oven to 180°C.
2. Spray a pie dish with non-stick spray.
3. Pour the apple slices into an oven-proof dish
   and smash them with a fork.
   → *optional*
4. Mix in the raisins and cinnamon.
5. In a large bowl, sift the flour, then add the
   sugar and baking powder.
6. In a separate bowl, beat the egg, then add it
   to the dry ingredients.
7. Mix the flour, sugar, baking powder and egg
   together.
8. Sprinkle the crumbly dough over the top of the
   apple.
9. Melt the margarine in the microwave.
10. Pour the margarine evenly over the top of the
    dough.
11. Sprinkle a little sugar on top.
12. Bake in the oven for 40 minutes, or until
    crispy-golden on top.
13. Serve with ice cream and custard.

If you're wondering what smudge is like, it's kind of like squishing together a piece of fudge and a brownie.

Totally the bomb-diggity! ←

HOOFIE-DUDE'S SMUDGE

Not only is Hoofie-dude a cool unicorn, but he is a cool baker.
He digs listening to his latest downloaded jams as he bakes. Hoofie-dude
has made a name for himself by his superb breakdancing, air-guitar playing
and smudge-baking skills. Be sure to listen to your favourite music while
trying this recipe. Also, why not have a go at some air guitar?

Ingredients

1 packet marie biscuits
1 egg
5ml vanilla essence
175g butter
2 cups icing sugar
2 tbsp cocoa powder
Non-stick spray

Method

1. Spray a glass dish with non-stick spray.
2. Break the marie biscuits into a bowl.
3. Beat the egg and vanilla essence in a separate bowl.
4. Melt the butter in a pot on a low heat on the stove.
5. Add the icing sugar and cocoa to the pot and whisk.
6. Take the pot off the stove.
7. Add the egg mixture.
8. Gently add the broken biscuits.
9. Mix together gently.
10. Pat the mixture into a glass dish with a spatula or wooden spoon.
11. Place in the fridge for 1 hour.
12. Turn the glass dish upside down on a bread board.
13. Cut the smudge into squares.

Dig in!

Colour me in!

27

SPRINKLES' ONE-EGG CAKE

Sprinkles, the unicorn, absolutely adores rainbows. She loves them so much that, believe or not, she eats them! The other thing she loves to eat is her spongy one-egg cake.

It is said that if you're ever lucky enough to touch a white unicorn, you'll be happy forever. Well, let me tell you, if you're ever lucky enough to eat a slice of this cake, you'll be beaming from ear to ear. You may even break out into a happy dance and fart rainbows.

Cake ←

Ingredients

→ at room temperature

100g butter
1 cup white sugar
1 egg
½ tsp vanilla essence
2 cups cake flour
¼ tsp salt
3 tsp baking powder
¾ cup milk
Non-stick spray

→ Icing

Ingredients

→ at room temperature

200g butter
1¼ cups icing sugar
1 tsp vanilla essence
100s and 1 000s colourful
cake sprinkles

Method *Cake*

1. Preheat the oven to 180°C.
2. Spray a cake tin with non-stick spray.
3. In a large bowl, cream the butter and sugar.
4. Beat the egg in a separate bowl.
5. Add the egg and vanilla essence to the butter and sugar. Beat until well mixed.
6. Add 1 cup of flour (don't forget to sift it), salt and baking powder. Mix.
7. Slowly add milk while mixing.
8. Add 2nd cup of flour (also sifted).
9. Beat together for 1 minute.
10. Pour the mixture into the cake tin.
11. Bake for about 40 minutes.
12. Once the cake is baked, place it on a rack to cool.

Here's something to do while you wait for your cake to bake:

- Think of a unicorn name for yourself.
- Set up a jumping course around the house. Pretend to be a unicorn and jump the course.
- Dye your hair pink, purple or blue. → *only joking!*
- Make the icing.

Method → *Icing*

1. Mix all of the ingredients together with an electric mixer, on a medium speed for 4 minutes, until it is light and fluffy, just like a cloud.
2. Spread the icing over the cake when it is cool.
3. Sprinkle 100s and 1 000s over the top. Slice and enjoy the wonders of unicorn baking.

P.S.
This recipe is also perfect for cupcakes. Just be sure to shorten the cooking time.

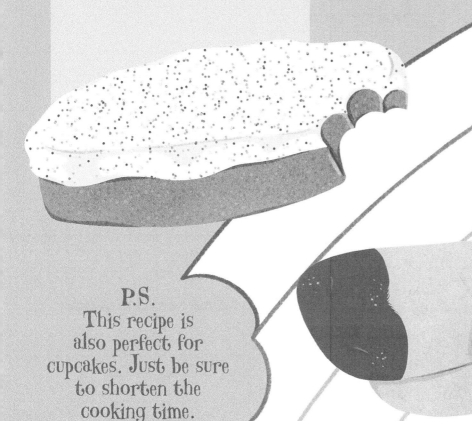

SPARKY'S FRIKKADELS

Makes 30 meatballs

Sparky is completely bonkers about frikkadels. He cooks his frikkadels with a blast of fire from his nose. Sadly, humans do not have the same super-power. While eating them, he gets so excited by the tasty flavour that he begins to bounce about like a crazy grasshopper. Then … he juggles the meaty balls!

→ not recommended that you try this!

Ingredients

1kg lean beef mince
1 packet oxtail soup powder
2 large white onions
1½ cups bread crumbs
1 500g carton buttermilk
1 tin tomato-and-onion mix
Salt and pepper, to taste

Grating an onion is certain to make you cry. Unfortunately, that can't be helped. It's an onion thing. Be careful not to grate the onion all of the way to the end – you may end up grating a finger or two. Ouch!

You have washed your hands, right?

Method *Meatballs*

1. Preheat the oven to 180°C.
2. Use your (clean) hands to crumble the mince into a mixing bowl. Season it (give it flavour) with salt and pepper.
3. Sprinkle the soup powder over the mince.
4. Grate 1 onion and add it to the mince.
   — Please note …
5. Add the bread crumbs to your mixture.
6. Add the buttermilk and mix it in with a fork.
7. Squish the mixture into balls.
8. Pack the balls into an oven dish or a large oven-proof pan. Add water until it is 1cm deep in the dish.
9. Place your dish in the oven and cook for 1½ hours or until your frikkadels are nicely browned. Turn your frikkadels after 1 hour of the cooking time.

Method *Tomato-and-onion sauce*

1. Fry 1 onion until golden brown.
2. Add the tin of tomato and onion.
3. Season with salt and pepper.
4. Serve with rice, tomato-and-onion sauce, and chutney.

DYNAMO'S ROAST CHICKEN

Dynamo doesn't have time for fussy or fancy meals. He has far more exciting things to do with his time, like:

* Blowing bigger and better flames.
* Practising his smoke-blowing animal art.
* Training for the Flying Olympics.
* Searching for treasure to sleep on.

You did know that dragons sleep on treasure, right?

Ingredients

1 whole defrosted chicken
Olive oil
Salt and pepper

Method

1. Preheat the oven to 180°C.
2. Dry the skin of the chicken with a paper towel. *Dry skin means crispy skin!*
3. Smother the chicken in olive oil.
4. Put the chicken in a roasting pan and sprinkle with salt and pepper.
5. Cook the chicken in the oven for 1½ hours, or until crispy and golden.
6. Let the chicken rest for 15 minutes before digging in.
7. Serve with your favourite vegetables.

And that's it! No fuss, no frills.

VALONDRI'S CONDENSED-MILK BISCUITS

Makes 50

Figuring out what sort of creature Valondri is can be a little confusing. Some say that she's a monster, others say she's a dinosaur, but since she can breathe a teeny, tiny bit of fire from her nose, let's call her a dragon. One whiff of her delicious biscuits is enough to make anyone salivate!

make your mouth water.

Ingredients

250g butter
at room temperature
1 cup brown sugar
½ tin of condensed milk
½ tsp vanilla essence
3¼ cups cake flour
2 tsp baking powder
Pinch of salt
Non-stick spray

Method

1. Preheat the oven to 180°C.
2. Spray a baking tray with non-stick spray.
3. In a large bowl, cream the butter and sugar.
4. Add the condensed milk and vanilla essence.
5. Beat well.
6. In a separate bowl, sift the flour, baking powder and salt.
7. Add all of the ingredients together.
8. Knead well.
9. Roll the batter into balls and place them on a baking sheet.
10. Flatten each ball with a fork.
11. Bake until golden (about 12–14 minutes).

Colour me in!

Be warned: Once you start eating these biscuits, it's almost impossible to stop! They're that good!

DODO-LICIOUS CHOCOLATE-CHIP COOKIES

Makes 24

Good news! The dodo isn't extinct! No way, nu-ah, nothing doing, not on your nelly. Dodos are still very much alive and thriving on Picadeeda Island. Yippee! And, boy oh boy, do they bake brilliant biscuits.

Ingredients

125g butter *at room temperature*

1 cup brown sugar

1 egg

½ tsp vanilla essence

1¾ cups self-raising flour

¼ tsp salt

Non-stick spray

150g chocolate chips

Method

1. Preheat the oven to 180°C.
2. Spray a baking tray with non-stick spray.
3. In a large bowl, cream the butter and sugar.
4. Lightly beat an egg and gradually add it to the butter and sugar.
5. Add the vanilla essence.
6. Sift the flour and salt into the mixture, and then blend the ingredients together.
7. Add chocolate chips and mix.
8. Roll into balls and press down lightly onto the baking tray with the palm of your hand.
9. Bake for 8–12 minutes.

FLAMBOYANT FLAMINGO RICE KRISPIES TREATS

Flamingos generally eat seeds, algae, tiny crabs and larvae, and they're pink in colour. Not the flamingos on Picadeeda Island! There, they are rainbow-coloured and spend their days snacking on their favourite Flamingo Fare!

Ingredients

1 ½ tbsp butter
10 large marshmallows
3 cups Rice Krispies cereal
Non-stick spray

Method

1. Line a baking tray with non-stick spray so the treats can be easily removed.
2. Melt the butter in a saucepan over a medium-low heat.
3. Add the marshmallows.
4. Keep stirring until the marshmallows are melted.
5. Remove from the stove and add the Rice Krispies.
6. Mix together.
7. Place gently into a baking tray.
8. Pat down lightly with a spoon and leave to set.
9. Cut into squares.

Why not be like a Picadeeda flamingo and try eating these treats while standing on one leg?

Nom, nom, nom!

CHIRPY AND TWITCH'S SHORTBREAD

Chirpy can always be found bopping around the river rocks with his best friend, Twitch. Their tails constantly bob up and down as they move in time to their chirping. They especially love to chirp while baking their delightful shortbread biscuits. Chirpy takes on the soprano (high) notes while Twitch chirps the bass. As cute as they are, their chirping does drive their island friends a little insane.

Try to see how long you can chirp before someone tells you to cut it out. *That is ... if you can chirp!*

Ingredients

180g cake flour
120g butter
1 tsp vanilla essence
60g castor sugar
Non-stick spray

Method

1. Preheat the oven to 180°C.
2. Spray a baking tray with non-stick spray.
3. Sift the flour into a mixing bowl.
4. Cut the butter into little cubes.
5. Add the butter to the flour. Rub the butter and the flour together with your cleanly washed fingers until the mixture becomes crumbly.
6. Add the vanilla essence and sugar. Mix it in until the mixture forms a ball.
7. Sprinkle a clean surface with flour.
8. Roll the dough out with a rolling pin to about ½ cm thick.
9. Use biscuit cutters to cut out shapes. Carefully lift the shapes and place them on the baking tray.
10. Re-roll the remaining dough and make more biscuits.
11. Bake in the oven for 12–15 minutes, or until they are a slightly golden.

Enjoy!

SCRUNCH'S PINWHEELS

Get ready for a rocking and rolling good time. Scrunch, along with all the trolls, lives in the mountain caves of Picadeeda Island. Scrunch can never remember anybody's name so he refers to everyone as "Buddy". Scrunch is a rather adorable troll and everyone kind of likes being referred to as his buddy.

Luckily, nobody minds.

Ingredients

**1 sheet ready-made
puff pastry
1 cup chutney
2 cups grated Cheddar
or Gouda cheese
Non-stick spray**

Method

1. Preheat oven to 200°C.
2. Spray a baking sheet with non-stick spray.
3. Unroll the pastry onto a lightly floured surface.
4. Spread chutney on the top of the pastry, then sprinkle the cheese evenly on top.
5. Roll up the pastry loosely.
6. Cut the roll into slices about 1½ cm thick.
7. Place each 'wheel' flat on a baking sheet.
8. Bake for about 12 minutes, until golden brown.
9. Stand back and admire your handiwork – but only for a moment.

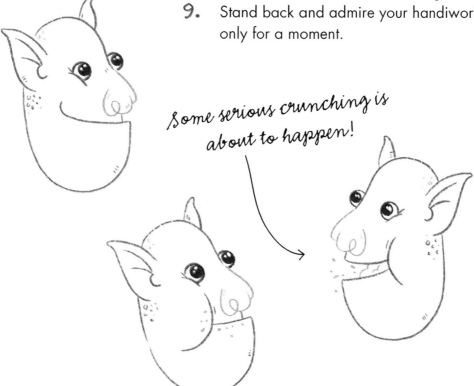

Some serious crunching is about to happen!

43

PLIP AND PLOP'S YUM-IN-THE-TUM SLIDERS

If you're into happy vibes, you've come to the right place. Because it's slider o'clock! These juicy sliders are made by siblings Plip and Plop.

Plip and Plop don't always get along. You can often here them arguing from their cave bedrooms. The squabbles get worse when they're tired, bored or … hungry! The family loves slider o'clock. This is the time when Plip and Plop are at their happiest – there isn't a squeak of a squabble. Plip makes the bread buns and Plop takes care of the patties. If you're ready for a good time, get started on these now!

BREAD BUNS BY PLIP

Makes 24

Ingredients

2 tbsp dry yeast
1 cup warm water
⅓ cup sunflower oil
¼ cup white sugar
1 egg
1 tsp salt
3½ cups cake flour
Non-stick spray

This dough is super sticky. The best way to work it is to wash your hands after kneading, and to then keep them well coated with flour.

Method

1. Preheat the oven to 180°C.
2. Spray a baking tray with non-stick spray.
3. In a large bowl, dissolve the yeast using the warm water.
4. Add the oil and sugar. Leave it to stand for 5 minutes.
5. Add the egg, salt and enough flour to form a dough.

Please note …

6. Knead until smooth and elastic, for about 3–5 minutes. Do not let it rise.
7. Roll the dough into balls.
8. Cover the tray and allow the dough to rest for 10 minutes.
9. Bake until golden brown – for 10–12 minutes.

Plip's bread buns may be enjoyed with any other filling: Peanut butter, jam, chicken and mayonnaise, cheese, Marmite, or even just plain butter.

BEEF PATTIES BY PLOP

Makes 24

Ingredients

½ onion
500g lean beef mince
1 egg
1 cup bread crumbs
½ tsp salt
½ tsp pepper
½ tsp mixed herbs
Sunflower oil

Method

1. Chop the onion finely and place it in a large mixing bowl.
2. Add the mince, egg, bread crumbs, salt, pepper and mixed herbs.
3. Squish everything together with your washed hands.
4. Roll the mince into little balls and press them flattish.
5. Heat the oil in a frying pan on the stove. About 1 cm deep.
6. Fry the patties on both sides, until the mince is well browned.
7. Place your patties on a sheet of kitchen paper towel, on a plate, to absorb excess oil.
8. Build your slider! Consider adding any of these items to your burger:
   - Cheese
   - Butter
   - Sliced tomatoes
   - Lettuce
   - Tomato sauce
   - Chutney
   - Mayonnaise
   - Gherkins
   - Avocado

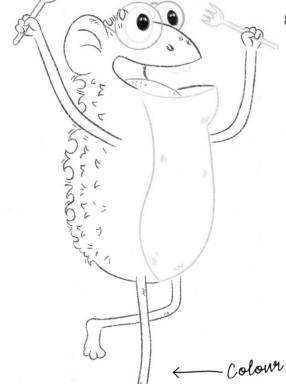

← Colour me in!

MAGICAL MERMAID MELTING MOMENTS

Makes 28

If you're keen to taste something that is dainty, delicate and divine, then this mermaid recipe is for you.

Ingredients

180g butter *at room temperature*
3 tbsp icing sugar
1½ cups cake flour
2 tbsp custard powder
Non-stick spray

Method

1. Preheat the oven to 180°C.
2. Spray a baking sheet with non-stick spray.
3. Cream the butter and sugar together in a bowl.
4. Sift the flour and custard powder on top of the butter and sugar.
5. Mix well.
6. Roll the batter into little balls and place them on the tray.
7. Press down on each ball with a fork.
8. Bake for 18 minutes.

NARAMA CHOCOLATE BROWNIES
Makes 16

Well, now you do!

Did you know that along the edge of Picadeeda Island there is a small frozen inlet? This is where Ned the Narama lives. He is a delightful, bright-orange, fluffy whale with a golden horn. His signature dish happens to be chocolate brownies.

You're certain to have a whale of a time baking these.

Ingredients

1 cup white or brown sugar
2 tbsp cocoa powder
1 tsp baking powder
Pinch of salt
1 tsp vanilla essence
2 eggs
¾ cup cake flour
½ cup butter → *melted*
Icing sugar *for dusting*

Method

1. Preheat the oven to 180°C.
2. Spray a square baking tin with non-stick spray.
3. Mix the sugar, cocoa, baking powder, salt and vanilla essence together in a bowl.
4. In a separate bowl, beat the eggs and then add them to the mixture. Mix with a wooden spoon until smooth.
5. Sift the flour on top of the mixture.
6. Add the melted butter. Mix thoroughly, using a wooden spoon. → *Do not use an electric beater.*
7. Spread the mixture into the baking tin.
8. Bake for 30 minutes.
9. Dust with icing sugar while still hot.
10. Cool and cut into squares.

Colour me in!

PURRMAID FISH FINGERS AND MASH

Purrmaids are real! Oh, joy! Oh, happiness! Purrmaids are half-cat, half-mermaid.

How magically marvellous!

Purring while eating this meal is highly recommended.

Ingredients

Fish fingers
↳ *However many you choose to eat*

1 potato → *or more*
1 tbsp butter
1 tbsp milk
Salt and pepper → *to taste*
Non-stick spray

Method

1. Preheat the oven to 220°C.
2. Apply non-stick spray to a baking tray.
3. Position the fish fingers on the tray and place it in the oven for 11 minutes.
4. Turn the fish fingers after 6 minutes.
5. Set a pot of water on the stove to boil.
6. Peel the potato/s and rinse in water.
7. Cut the potato/s into quarters with a knife.
8. Place the potato/s in the water. The water level should just cover the quarters.
9. When the water begins to boil, turn the temperature down low.
10. The potatoes are cooked when you can easily stick a fork in them.
11. Drain the water from the pot.
12. Mash the potato in a bowl using a masher.
13. Add butter and milk until the potato/s are soft and creamy.
14. Season with salt and pepper to taste.
15. Serve with peas and tomato sauce or mayonnaise.

GIROLPHIN'S TUNA PASTA

Makes 16 servings

Girolphin is an absolute delight. After he has eaten his tuna pasta, he can be spotted anywhere off the coast of Picadeeda Island having a good time. His favourite activities include:

- Blowing bubble rings from his blowhole.
- Playing hide-and-seek with whales.
- Seeing how high he can jump.
- Delivering gifts for the island creatures ⟶ *free of charge.*
- Giggling a lot.

Ingredients

1 cup pasta shells
3 cups water
1 apple
1 tbsp mayonnaise
170g tin tuna
Pinch of salt
Pinch of pepper

Method

1. Add pasta shells to a pot of boiling water. Don't cover the pot. Boil rapidly for about 10 minutes, or until tender.
2. Drain the hot water in a colander.
3. Rinse the pasta under cold water.
4. Dice your apple ⟶ *cut it into little cubes.*
5. In a bowl, mix the pasta with all your other ingredients.
6. Place it in the fridge and then eat it cold – or warmish.
   ⟶ *however you prefer it.*

Please note: Pinching should only be done in baking. Pinching humans or animals isn't very nice. :-)

OODLE'S MACARONI CHEESE

Attention, all pasta fans!

It gives me great pleasure to highly recommend the cooking and eating of Oodle's Noodles. They're the squishiest, delishiest (not a word), slurpiest, sloppiest, slipperiest, squelchiest, schmooziest food on earth.

Ingredients

2 cups uncooked macaroni noodles
8 cups water
2 tbsp butter
2 tbsp cake flour
2 cups milk
2 cups grated Cheddar cheese *or Gouda*
2 pinches of salt
2 pinches of pepper
2–3 tomatoes
1 pack of bacon

Method

1. Preheat the oven to 180°C.
2. Add the macaroni to a pot of boiling water. Don't cover the pot. Boil rapidly for about 10 minutes, or until tender.
3. Drain and rinse the pasta under cold water.
4. In a pan, melt the butter. Mix in the flour. Slowly add the milk and stir constantly until you have a creamy sauce. Add 1 cup of grated cheese. Stir until the cheese is melted.
5. Add salt and pepper.
6. Mix the sauce with the macaroni and place it in an oven-proof dish.
7. Layer 1 cup of grated cheese, sliced tomatoes and diced bacon on top.
8. Place in the oven for 40 minutes.
9. Serve with tomato sauce.

SLOTHERPILLAR SCONES

Makes 12

Slotherpillars are purple with red spots, and they have wings! Sadly, the wings are too small to allow them to fly, but they do help to keep them cool. They are sort of like a built-in body fan.

Ingredients

4 cups cake flour
8 tsp baking powder
1 tsp salt
2 eggs
½ cup sunflower oil
1½ cups water
Non-stick spray

Method

1. Preheat the oven to 180°C.
2. Apply non-stick spray to the muffin pan.
3. In a large bowl, sift the flour and add the baking powder and salt. Mix together.
4. In a separate bowl, beat together the eggs, oil and water.
5. Add the ingredients together and mix.
6. Spoon the mixture into the muffin pan.
7. Bake in the oven for 30 minutes.

Yum!

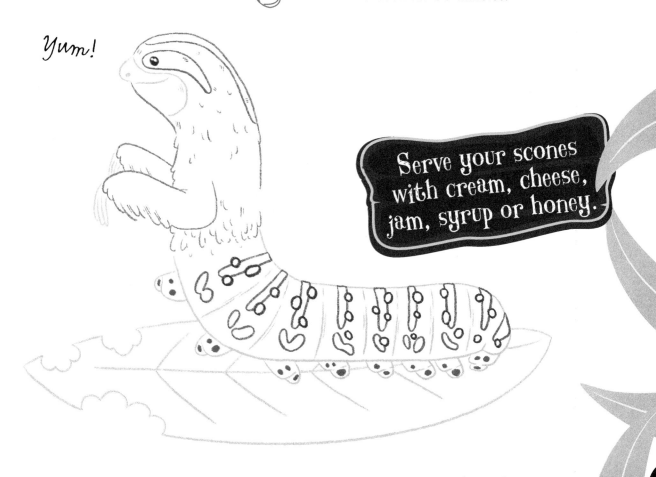

Serve your scones with cream, cheese, jam, syrup or honey.

GOLINGALEE MINI PIZZAS

Makes 12

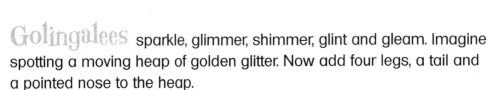

Golingalees sparkle, glimmer, shimmer, glint and gleam. Imagine spotting a moving heap of golden glitter. Now add four legs, a tail and a pointed nose to the heap.

   Ka-ching! You have a Picadeeda Golingalee.

Ingredients

1½ cups cake flour
2 tsp baking powder
Pinch of salt
1 tbsp olive oil
½ cup warm water
Tomato sauce
Ham
Cheese
Non-stick spray

Method

1. Preheat the oven to 220°C.
2. Spray a baking tray with non-stick spray.
3. Sift the flour, baking powder and salt into a large mixing bowl and stir.
4. Make a well in the middle and add the oil.
5. Pour in the water a little at a time and mix until you have created a soft dough.
6. Use your hands to squash the dough into a ball and then knead it for a minute or two.
7. Sprinkle a little flour on a clean surface and roll out the dough until it's ½ cm thick.
8. Use a circle cookie cutter to press eight circles out of the dough. Lay them on the baking tray.
9. Keep re-rolling and cutting the remaining dough.
10. Use a teaspoon to spoon tomato sauce onto each pizza. Spread the sauce with the back of the spoon.
11. Cut the ham into little squares.
12. Grate the cheese.

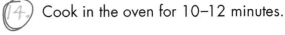 *Watch out for your fingers.*

13. Add a few pieces of ham and a sprinkling of cheese onto each pizza.
14. Cook in the oven for 10–12 minutes.

Try this salad, and you too can save the day, the spiky-hero way.

SPIKY-PUFF'S SALAD

Spiky-puff is the protector of the island. If anyone is in any sort of trouble, he's there in a flash. Spiky-puff is sort of like Superman, except spikier. He gets his super-strength from eating salad.

Ingredients

1 cucumber
1 yellow bulb pepper
Lettuce
Cherry tomatoes
Wooden skewers

Method

1. Slice the cucumber into slices about 1 cm thick.
2. Slice and dice the pepper.
3. Tear the lettuce into pieces.
4. Gently slide the salad items onto the skewers, creating interesting patterns.
5. Optional salad items include:
   - Gherkins
   - Feta cheese
   - Olives
   - Onions.

← Colour me in!

Note: This also works brilliantly with fruit.

CONVERSION TABLE

Teaspoons (tsp)

2ml	¼ tsp
3ml	½ tsp
5ml	1 tsp
10ml	2 tsp
15ml	3 tsp

Tablespoons (tbsp)

15ml	1 tbsp
30ml	2 tbsp
45ml	3 tbsp

Cups

60ml	¼ cup
80ml	⅓ cup
125ml	½ cup
160ml	⅔ cup
200ml	¾ cup
250ml	1 cup
375ml	1½ cups
500ml	2 cups
750ml	3 cups
1 litre	4 cups

BASIC INGREDIENTS

	¼ cup	⅓ cup	½ cup	¾ cup	1 cup
Flour	35g	45g	70g	110g	140g
Sugar	50g	65g	100g	160g	200g
Icing sugar	35g	45g	70g	100g	130g
Margarine and butter	60g	75g	120g	185g	230g